Charles Dickens

retold by Jenny Dooley

Express Publishing

Published by Express Publishing

Liberty House, Greenham Business Park,
Newbury, Berkshire RG19 6HW, United Kingdom
Tel.: (0044) 1635 817 363 – Fax: (0044) 1635 817 463
email: inquiries@expresspublishing.co.uk
www.expresspublishing.co.uk

© Jenny Dooley, 2003

Design & Illustration © Express Publishing, 2003

Colour Illustrations: Nathan & Stone

First published 2003
Published in this edition 2012
Sixth impression 2017

Made in EU

ISBN 978-1-84466-149-7

Contents

Introductory Lesson

Before Reading

1 **Work in pairs. Answer the following questions:**
   a Look at the front cover of the book. What can you see in the picture?
   b In which period of time do you think the story is set?
   c Read the blurb on the back cover. Why do you think children became thieves in the past?
   d Look at the chapter titles. In which chapter do you think Oliver had the most difficult time? Why?

2 **Look at the following pictures. How do you think they are connected to the story?**

handcuffs

a coffin

a pistol

socks

bread

coins

a handkerchief

3 Read the information about *Charles Dickens* and answer the questions that follow.

Charles Dickens

 Charles Dickens was born in Portsmouth, England, on February 7th 1812 and spent his childhood in London and Kent. He started school when he was nine years old, but had to stop soon afterwards because his father owed money and was sent to prison. This meant that Dickens had to go to work to support himself. His first job was in a shoe polish factory and he used this experience when he wrote his novels. In 1827, he started to work as a legal clerk. He learned shorthand*, which he later used when he became a reporter. He married Catherine Hogarth in 1836. "The Pickwick Papers" was published a year later and "Oliver Twist" was published in 1838.

Throughout his adult life, Dickens was concerned for the poor people in England and in his later life, he gave a number of talks and lectures on social conditions in an effort to improve their lives. He died on June 9th 1870, and is buried in Westminster Abbey, London.

---

* Shorthand: a quick way of writing, using signs instead of words or syllables.

a Where was Charles Dickens born?

b How old was he when he started school?

c Why did he have to start work when he was still a child?

d What jobs did Dickens have before he started writing novels?

e When was *"Oliver Twist"* published?

f What interested Dickens all his life?

g Where is Charles Dickens buried?

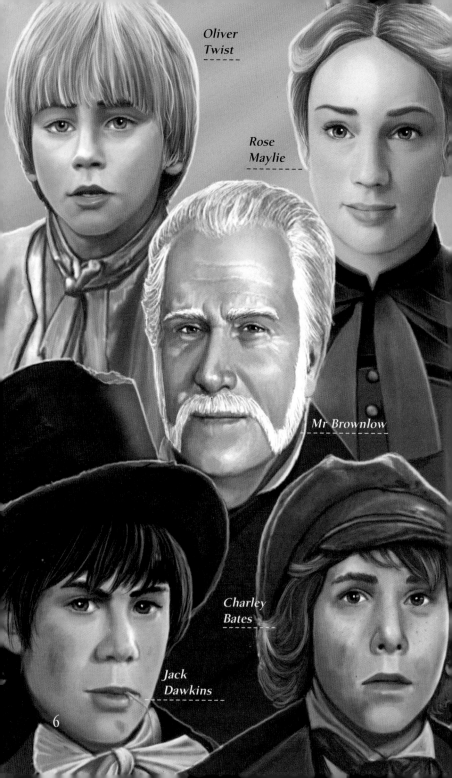

Oliver
Twist
- - - - - -

Rose
Maylie
- - - - - - - - -

Mr Brownlow
- - - - - - - - - - - -

Charley
Bates
- - - - -

Jack
Dawkins
- - - - - - - -

6

Edward
Leeford
(Monks)

Fagin

Nancy

Bill
Sikes

7

At the Workhouse

Many years ago in England, there were special places called workhouses, where poor people went to live when they had no money or work, no family or friends to help them and when they had nowhere else to go. Life in the workhouse was hard for the poor people and they went there only if they had no hope of a better life.

One cold, dark night a young woman arrived in a strange town. She was pregnant and very tired and she fell down in the street. No one knew who she was or where she came from so the people who found her took her to the workhouse.

An old woman called Sally put the girl to bed, and then sat down by the fire to wait for the doctor. Suddenly the girl cried out and looked at Sally with eyes full of pain and fear.

"Don't be afraid, dear," said the old woman. "I've had thirteen children and I've often helped the doctor when a child was born in the workhouse. Your child will be born soon, but don't worry! The doctor's on his way!"

Something was troubling the young woman. She tried to take off the gold chain she was wearing around her neck. Sally helped her and then the girl put the chain, which had a locket with the name 'Agnes' on it, into Sally's hand.

"Take these things ... please, keep them safe for my child ... I'm very sick! I don't think I'll live to see the baby."

"Don't talk like that!" said Sally. "Close your eyes now and try to rest. You'll need all your strength for the birth."

Sally put the things into her pocket and just at that moment the doctor arrived. Soon a baby boy was born. The young mother lay in bed, very tired and very sick. When the baby began to cry the girl opened her eyes and tried to sit up.

"Let me see my baby before I die."

"Come," said the doctor kindly, "you must not talk of dying."

He put the baby in the mother's arms.

"His name is Oliver," she said, then kissed the child and fell back on the pillow.

The doctor and Sally did everything they could, but it was too late. The girl was dead.

"Well, Sally, I'm afraid there's nothing more I can do here," said the doctor sadly to the old woman. "Where did she come from?"

"I don't know, but she walked a long way to get here. Her shoes were worn out."

"And the baby's father?"

"We don't know anything about him. Maybe he's dead. She arrived here alone."

"Poor girl," said the doctor and he sighed as he put on his hat and gloves. Then he said goodnight to Sally and went home.

When Sally was alone again she sat by the fire with the baby in a cradle at her feet. She took the locket out of her pocket and for a long time she looked at it and at the sleeping baby. There were two small locks of hair in the locket, one fair, like the girl's and one dark. There was also a gold wedding ring inside it. At last, she put them back into her pocket and shook her head sadly.

"Poor baby … I'm sorry, but I'm going to keep these things and sell them myself. Then I can have a bit of money now that I'm old. I've lived in the workhouse for fifty years and life here is very hard."

Children didn't go to the workhouse until they were nine years old. Before that they lived in another house, where somebody looked after them and received money to pay for their food. Oliver went to live in such a house with Mrs Mann, an old woman who kept most of the money for herself and didn't take good care of the babies and children. For the first nine years of his life Oliver lived there and during that time he never heard a kind word and he never had enough to eat.

On Oliver's ninth birthday, Mr Bumble, a big fat man who wore a uniform and carried a big stick, came to take him to the men's workhouse. Mr Bumble helped to manage the workhouse. He had a bad temper and he was very strict. If anyone in the workhouse did anything wrong, Mr Bumble hit them with his stick, so everybody was afraid of him, especially the children.

One of his jobs was to give surnames to the babies who had no father. No one knew the name of Oliver's father so Mr Bumble gave him the surname 'Twist'.

Life in the workhouse was very hard and the boys were always hungry. The food was always the same—a bowl of soup, which was mostly water, and on Sundays a small piece of bread. The master of the workhouse served the soup from a big pot, and he gave just one bowl to each boy. The boys became so hungry that one day they decided that someone must ask for more. They thought that if one boy got more soup, they could all get more. They chose Oliver.

The master served the soup as usual and the boys ate it quickly. They licked their fingers and then looked at Oliver and the big pot of soup.

"Go on then! Go on!" they whispered and pushed Oliver with their elbows.

Oliver was afraid, but he stood up, picked up his empty bowl, and walked slowly to the master. There was complete silence. All the boys were waiting, hopefully.

Oliver held out his bowl.

"Please, sir. I want some more."

The master couldn't believe his ears. He looked at Oliver's pale, thin face and the empty bowl.

"What???"

"Please, sir, I'm hungry. I want some more," said Oliver again.

"Mr Bumble!" shouted the master, and he hit Oliver on the head with his big soup spoon. All the boys waited to see what happened.

Mr Bumble appeared at the door.

"What's the matter, Master?"

"Oliver Twist wants more soup!"

Mr Bumble's face went red and he looked very angry.

"What? It's not possible! No one has ever asked for more! Oliver Twist, you are a bad, ungrateful boy!"

He picked up poor Oliver by his shirt collar and began to shake him and beat him with his big stick. Then he took him away and locked him in the cellar. Oliver was cold and frightened and he cried all night.

The next morning Mr Bumble put a notice on the door of the workhouse.

Do you want a boy
to learn a useful job?
We will give £ 5
to anyone
who takes him.

Life with Mr Sowerberry

For a week Oliver stayed alone in the cold, dark cellar, and it was the worst week of his life so far. Every morning Mr Bumble unlocked the door, took Oliver into the room where the boys were eating, and beat him, while the boys watched. Then he locked Oliver in the room again. Poor Oliver cried all day and, at night he couldn't sleep because he was cold, unhappy ... and hungry.

One morning, at the end of that week, Mr Bumble saw Mr Sowerberry, the coffin maker, outside the workhouse. Mr Sowerberry was a tall, thin man who always wore black clothes because of his job. He often came to the workhouse because so many poor people died there and so he knew Mr Bumble well. The two men began to chat, and then Mr Bumble pointed to the notice on the workhouse door.

"Mr Sowerberry, do you know anyone who wants a boy—and five pounds?"

Mr Sowerberry thought for a few moments.

"I think I'll take him, Mr Bumble. I need a boy to work in my shop."

They went inside to make the arrangements.

That evening Mr Bumble unlocked the cellar door and told Oliver the news. Oliver said nothing. He just pulled the cap down over his eyes to hide his tears, and followed Mr Bumble through the streets to the coffin-maker's shop.

Mr Sowerberry was waiting for them. There was only the light from one small candle so the room was dark and gloomy. A finished coffin lay on a table in the middle of the room and pieces of wood stood against the walls. Mr Sowerberry smiled at Oliver and then called his wife.

"Mrs Sowerberry, will you come here for a moment, my dear?"

Mrs Sowerberry was a small, thin woman with an angry face. Oliver thought she looked like a fox. She looked at him and Oliver bowed politely.

"Hmm ... he's very small," she said, at last.

"Yes, he **is** small," agreed Mr Bumble, "but he'll grow, ma'am."

"Oh yes, he'll grow all right ... on our food and drink! Get downstairs, you little bag of bones!"

She pushed Oliver down some stairs into a dark little kitchen where a servant girl was working.

"Charlotte, give this boy those bits of meat the dog didn't eat."

For the first time in his life, Oliver tasted meat. He ate the dog's food hungrily, and then Mrs Sowerberry said,

"Your bed's under the shop counter. There's nowhere else, so enjoy sleeping in there—with the coffins!"

She laughed and left Oliver alone. He was very frightened and hardly slept all night.

Early in the morning Oliver heard someone kicking the door and shouting,

"Open the door!"

Oliver opened the door and a big boy walked into the shop.

"I am Mister Noah Claypole, and you must do what I tell you," said the boy. "Now take the shutters down and hurry up!"

He kicked Oliver as he walked past.

The work was hard but Mr Sowerberry was kind to Oliver. When Noah noticed this, he got jealous. He was always nasty to Oliver and made his life very difficult. One day the two boys were in the kitchen together. Noah wanted to make Oliver cry. He pulled his hair, pinched his ears, and said all the horrible things he could think of. But Oliver did not cry.

"How's your mother?" asked Noah.

"She's dead."

Noah thought Oliver was ready to cry, so he continued.

"I heard your mother was a bad woman."

Oliver's face went red and he jumped to his feet and hit Noah so hard that the big boy fell down. Noah began to shout.

"Charlotte! Mrs Sowerberry! Help! Oliver's murdering me!"

The two women ran into the kitchen and they both hit Oliver. Charlotte locked him in the coal cellar until Mr Sowerberry came home. When Mrs Sowerberry told him what happened, he beat Oliver too, and sent him to bed without any supper.

Alone with the gloomy coffins, Oliver burst into tears. He cried for a long time but at last he had an idea and wiped his eyes. He decided to run away to London and look for work there. As soon as it was light, he took all the things he owned—a shirt, two pairs of socks, a piece of bread and a penny—and tied them up in a big handkerchief. Then he quietly opened the door and set off.

On the Streets of London

For a whole week, Oliver walked during the day and slept in the fields at night. Some kind people gave him food and water. At last, he arrived in London. His feet were bleeding and he sat down on a doorstep to rest. He was wondering what to do when he heard a voice.

"Hello, there! What's the matter?"

Oliver looked up and saw a strange boy wearing a man's coat, which reached almost to the ground, and an old top hat.

"I'm very hungry and tired," said Oliver. "I've been on the road for seven days."

"Come with me and I'll buy you something to eat," said the boy. "My name is Jack Dawkins, but they call me the Artful Dodger."

After a meal of bread and cold meat, Jack Dawkins began to ask questions.

"Have you got any money?"

"No."

"Do you know anyone here?"

"No."

"I suppose you want somewhere to sleep tonight, don't you?"

"Oh, yes, please."

"I know an old man who can help you. Come with me."

Oliver could not believe his luck, and followed his new friend gratefully.

It was late when the two boys stopped outside the door of an old house in one of the poorest areas of the city. Jack went in quickly and Oliver followed him up the stairs into a big room at the top of the house.

The walls and ceiling were black with smoke and dirt. An old man with long, greasy red hair was cooking some meat in a pan over the fire, and a few young boys were sitting around a table.

"Mr Fagin, meet my friend, Oliver Twist!" said Jack.

The old man smiled, showing long, yellow teeth like a rat, and shook Oliver's hand. The boys all jumped up and shook Oliver's hand too. One boy took his cap, another his handkerchief, and a third checked his pockets.

The old man laughed and hit the boys playfully with the fork. Oliver sat down at the table with the other boys and looked around the room. A lot of colourful silk handkerchiefs were hanging on a line across the room. Oliver stared at them curiously. They looked too clean for that dirty room.

"Ah, you're admiring our handkerchiefs," said Fagin. "We've just washed them, my dear!"

He laughed again and all the boys laughed, too. Oliver didn't know why they were laughing, but he thought they were all very cheerful and friendly. After supper Jack showed him where to sleep—a mattress on the floor—and Oliver fell asleep at once.

The next morning Oliver woke up late and Fagin told him that the other boys were at work. Soon Jack and his friend, Charley Bates, came back. Jack gave Fagin two well-made wallets, and Charley had four silk handkerchiefs.

Fagin showed the things to Oliver.

"Look, Oliver, what clever boys they are. Would you like to learn to come home every day with wallets and handkerchiefs like these, hmm?"

"Oh yes, sir, if you'll teach me!"

Fagin and the boys laughed loudly, then they began to play a game. Fagin put some things into his pockets and the boys tried to take them out secretly. If Fagin felt a hand in his pocket, or saw one of the boys, Fagin was the winner. If the boys got the things without Fagin noticing, then they won the game. Oliver watched the boys carefully and soon he wanted to play, too. He learned quickly and Fagin was pleased.

A few days later, Fagin let Oliver go out with Jack and Charley. For a long time they walked around slowly, then suddenly Jack stopped. He pointed towards an old gentleman, standing outside a bookshop and whispered,

"He'll do!"

"Perfect!" agreed Charley.

Oliver didn't understand. He couldn't see anything special about the old gentleman. He was reading a book from the stall outside the shop and didn't seem to notice anything around him. Jack and Charley walked slowly towards him, then, quick as a flash, Jack pulled the handkerchief out of the old man's pocket and the two boys disappeared round the corner.

It was then that Oliver understood that Jack and Charley were thieves. He turned to run away but the old gentleman saw him and realised his handkerchief was not in his pocket.

"Stop thief!" he shouted, and soon a crowd of people was running after Oliver, all shouting "Stop thief!"

Oliver was terrified. He ran like the wind, but suddenly he slipped and fell. The crowd stood round him and the old gentleman looked down at him sadly.

"Yes, I'm afraid this is the boy."

Chapter 3

At that moment the man from the bookshop arrived.

"This boy is not the thief," he explained. "I saw everything from my shop! Two other boys stole the handkerchief!"

The old gentleman looked at Oliver's pale face and his innocent, frightened eyes.

"This boy is ill! Get a carriage. I'm taking him to my home."

Oliver closed his eyes and remembered nothing more.

Oliver Meets Mr Brownlow

When Oliver opened his eyes again he was in a clean, comfortable bed and an old lady was sitting near him.

"Where am I? Who are you?" he asked.

"You're in Mr Brownlow's house. I'm Mrs Bedwin, the housekeeper. You've been very ill for many days. Lie quietly now, dear, or you'll be ill again."

She stroked his hair and gave him a cool drink.

A few days later Oliver was well enough to get up. He sat downstairs in Mrs Bedwin's sitting room and looked at the picture of a young lady on the wall.

"Do you like that picture, dear?"

"Yes. The lady's face is so beautiful, but her eyes look sad."

"If the picture makes you sad, you mustn't look at it. I'll move your chair so that you can't see it."

She moved Oliver's chair to the opposite side of the room, below the picture. At that moment Mr Brownlow came in.

"How are you, my dear?" he asked Oliver.

"Very well now, thank you, sir."

Mr Brownlow smiled at Oliver, then suddenly his face changed. He opened his eyes wide and stared at the picture above Oliver's chair.

"Mrs Bedwin, what's this? Look at the boy's face! Look at the picture!"

Oliver's face was exactly like the face in the picture!

The next day, when he got up, Oliver looked for the picture, but it wasn't there. Mrs Bedwin noticed him looking at the wall.

"I've taken the picture away because it made you sad. When you're well again, I'll put it back."

Oliver was happy at Mr Brownlow's house. The kind old man bought new clothes for him and Mrs Bedwin gave him good food. One evening Mr Brownlow wanted to see him. So, Oliver washed his face, Mrs Bedwin combed his hair, and then he knocked at the door of Mr Brownlow's study. This was a pleasant room, full of books. Mr Brownlow was sitting at a table by the window, reading.

"Come in and sit down, Oliver. I want to talk seriously to you."

"Oh, please, sir. Don't tell me you're going to send me away!" said Oliver, and his eyes filled with tears.

"No, my dear child, if you're a good boy I'll never send you away. I want to hear your story. Tell me the truth and don't be afraid."

Oliver just started to tell Mr Brownlow his story when they heard a knock at the door. It was Mr Brownlow's friend, Mr Grimwig. Mr Grimwig was a fat old man who walked slowly with a stick. He didn't like boys.

"Hello! What's that?" he said when he saw Oliver.

"This is Oliver Twist, the boy I told you about. He was just telling me his story."

Mr Grimwig put his head on one side and looked at Oliver out of the corner of his eye.

"Don't trust that boy, Mr Brownlow. He'll tell you a pack of lies, or I'll eat my hat!"

"I **do** trust him, Grimwig."

At that moment Mrs Bedwin came in with some books.

"Tell the boy who brought them to wait," said Mr Brownlow.

"I want to send some books back to the shop."

"It's too late, sir, he's gone."

"Why don't you let Oliver take the books?" said Mr Grimwig.

"Oh yes, let me go, sir!"

Mr Brownlow didn't want Oliver to go out alone but he wanted to show Mr Grimwig that Oliver was a good boy and that he trusted him.

"Very well. Oliver, take these books and this money and bring me ten shillings change."

"Yes sir, thank you! I'll run all the way!"

Oliver ran out happily with the books and the money.

Mr Brownlow looked at the clock.

"He'll be back in … twenty minutes!"

"Do you really think he'll come back?" said Mr Grimwig. "The boy has new clothes, five pounds and some books. He'll go straight back to his friends, the thieves, and laugh at you. If that boy comes back here tonight, I'll eat my hat!"

Twenty minutes passed, then half an hour. It grew dark and Mrs Bedwin lit the gaslights. She sent the servants out twenty times to look for Oliver.

In Mr Brownlow's study the two old men sat in silence and looked at the clock. Oliver didn't come home.

Kidnapped

When Jack and Charley went home without Oliver, Fagin was very angry. He was shouting and beating the boys with his big stick when a man and a woman came in. They were Bill Sikes and his wife, Nancy. Bill was about thirty-five, tall and well-built, and Nancy had rosy cheeks and long, curly hair. Bill's dirty white dog followed them in.

"What's all this noise? What's going on in here?" asked Bill.

Fagin explained the problem.

"These stupid boys have lost Oliver and I'm afraid he will tell the police we're thieves. We must find him before he talks!"

"Nancy can help us. The police don't know she works with us."

Fagin cheered up.

"Yes, Nancy, my dear, you can go to the police station! Tell them you've lost your little brother Oliver, and find out where he is."

So, Nancy put on a clean, white apron and a straw bonnet and pretended to cry. She wiped her eyes with the corner of her apron and they all laughed. Then, Nancy left to see what she could find out. Soon she was back with some news.

"Oliver fell down in the street and an old gentleman took him home. This old man likes reading and buys lots of books."

"Well done, my dear!" cried Fagin. "Bill and Nancy! Watch the bookshop and sooner or later we'll find Oliver."

So, on the evening that Oliver went to the bookshop, Bill and Nancy were waiting for him. As soon as they saw him, Nancy started shouting.

"Oliver, you bad boy! Where have you been? Our mother is so worried!"

"You young devil! Aren't you ashamed? And what have you got there? Stolen books, eh? And money! That's mine!"

Bill snatched the money out of Oliver's hand and put it in his pocket. Oliver cried for help and tried to escape, but it was no use. Bill and Nancy held both his hands tightly and dragged him along the street, while the dog ran behind, growling.

Soon they arrived at Fagin's house.

"Oliver, my dear! You're looking very well … what have you got for us—books?"

"I don't care what you do to me, but please send the books back to Mr Brownlow! He's waiting for me and he'll think I've stolen them!"

Fagin laughed.

"That's right! He'll think you're a thief! Excellent!"

This was too much for Oliver. He rushed towards the door shouting.

"Help! Help!"

"Not so fast, young man!"

Fagin grabbed Oliver and picked up his stick. He was very angry.

"So, you want to run away again … you want to go to the police, eh? I'll teach you not to do that!"

He raised the stick to hit Oliver but Nancy jumped forward, snatched it out of his hand and threw it into the fire. She was angry, too.

"You've got the boy back, Fagin, but I won't let you hurt him!"

For the next few days, Fagin told Oliver terrible stories about the things that happened to boys who tried to run away or go to the police for help. Oliver was scared.

One night Fagin went to visit Bill Sikes. The two men sat down and began to talk about a house they wanted to rob.

"We can't get into the house, Fagin! There's only one window without bars and it's too small for a man to get through!"

"Hmm ... could a boy get in?"

"Yes ... if he was a very small, thin boy."

"Well ... Oliver's very small and thin, Bill. He can help us!"

The following evening Fagin got ready to go out.

"Oliver, Nancy will take you to Bill's house tonight."

"To ... to stay there?"

"No, my dear, we don't want to lose you!"

The old man laughed, and then suddenly his face became serious.

"Oliver, Bill Sikes is a dangerous man, so don't do anything to make him angry. He's not afraid of blood! Now, here's a candle and a book to read while you're waiting for Nancy."

When Oliver was alone, he began to read a book full of horrible stories about thieves, murderers and other criminals. By the time Nancy came to get him, he was terrified.

Nancy looked worried and her face was pale. She sat down near the fire and for a few minutes she did not move or speak. Then, suddenly she turned to Oliver and whispered quickly.

"Listen to me, Oliver. Do what Bill tells you. Don't shout or cry or try to escape. If you do, he'll kill both of us!"

She took his hand and soon they arrived at Bill's house. Bill was sitting down and a pistol was on the table in front of him.

"Come here," he said to Oliver and pointed to the pistol. "Do you know what this is?"

"Yes."

"Now, this is a bullet and this is gun-powder."

Bill loaded the pistol carefully as he spoke.

"It's loaded now, see?"

He held the pistol to Oliver's head.

"Well, if you speak one word while we're out, this bullet is for **you**! Understand?"

"Ye-yes, sir!"

Bill pushed the boy away, laughing at his pale face.

"Good! Now, let's have some supper and go to bed. We've got to get up very early tomorrow."

The Robbery

The next day was wet and cold. Oliver and Bill Sikes got up early and travelled all day. It was late in the evening when they arrived at a lonely, ruined cottage in the country, where Bill's friend, Toby Crackit, was waiting for them. He had long, red hair and thin legs and wore a lot of big rings on his dirty fingers.

They waited in the cottage until midnight. Then the two men went out and took Oliver with them. He tried to run away but they held his hands tightly.

"Be quiet! Remember the pistol, my boy!" said Bill.

It was cold and foggy as they were walking through the streets of a small village. Finally, they stopped outside a house with a big wall around it. They climbed over the wall and walked silently to the back of the house where they found one very small window open.

"Right, Oliver. I'm going to lift you in there and ..."

When Oliver realised that the thieves wanted him to help them rob the house, he fell down on his knees.

"I can't help you steal! Please let me go!"

Bill pulled out the pistol but Toby stopped him.

"Don't be a fool, Bill. If he says another word, I'll hit him on the head—that makes no noise."

"... when you get inside, go and open the front door for us. And be careful! I'm watching you!"

Oliver decided to shout for help as soon as he was in the house. He didn't want to be a thief. He took a step forward and then heard Bill's voice.

"Back! Come back!"

A man appeared at the open storeroom door holding a gun.

There was a bang and a flash of light. Oliver felt a pain in his arm and fell back. Bill grabbed him and pulled him through the window. Then he saw that Oliver's arm was covered in blood.

"They've shot him!"

But Toby Crackit was already running away towards some trees. Bill followed, carrying Oliver.

"Stop, you coward! Help me with the boy!"

They reached the trees and saw men with guns and dogs running out of the house towards them.

"Drop the boy and run!"

Bill thought for a moment, then dropped Oliver under a tree and the two thieves disappeared into the darkness.

A cold rain began to fall. All night Oliver lay under the tree without moving and his clothes turned red with blood. The bitter cold woke him up early in the morning. He opened his eyes with a cry of pain—his arm hurt badly. He tried to sit up. In the distance he could see a big house and he decided to ask for help there. He stood up with difficulty and staggered towards the house. Finally, tired and weak, he reached the house. He knocked at the door, then fainted on the doorstep.

At the same moment, the servants of the house were all in the kitchen, talking. Two of them, Mr Giles and Brittles were telling the others about the thieves who tried to rob the house in the night. Everyone was afraid when they heard the knock at the door. Mr Giles and Brittles went together to open the door, but instead of the dangerous robber they were expecting, they saw only a little boy, covered in blood, lying on the doorstep. They picked him up and brought him into the house.

"Miss! I've got him!" shouted Mr Giles. "It's the thief I shot last night! Do you want to see him?"

A girl's voice answered from upstairs.

"No, wait! Let me speak to my aunt."

A moment later her sweet voice was heard again.

"Giles, bring him upstairs and put him to bed. Brittles, go and fetch the doctor."

Giles carried Oliver upstairs to an empty bedroom. Very soon, Dr Losberne arrived and the servants ran up and down the stairs with hot water and bandages. About an hour later, Dr Losberne came downstairs to speak to the two ladies of the house— Mrs Maylie, an old lady, and Rose, a young girl of seventeen. Rose was also an orphan, just like Oliver, and Mrs Maylie took her in when she was a young child.

"Have you seen this thief yet, Mrs Maylie?" asked the doctor.

"No."

"I think you should. He's not as dangerous as you think," said the doctor with a smile.

The two ladies gasped in surprise when they saw Oliver, asleep in the bed.

"What's this? Surely such a small child can't be a thief!" cried Mrs Maylie.

Rose ran to the bed and her eyes filled with tears. She stroked Oliver's hair and turned to her aunt.

"Oh, Aunt! I don't believe he's a bad boy really. Maybe he's a poor orphan who never knew a mother's love. Can't he stay here? We can take care of him!"

"Of course he can stay!"

She turned to Dr Losberne.

"Doctor, what can we do to save him?"

44   As she spoke these words, Oliver Twist smiled in his sleep.

A Home for Oliver

Oliver stayed at the house until spring. When he was well and strong again, everyone moved to a beautiful cottage in the country. Life there was quiet and peaceful.

Every morning Oliver got up early to pick flowers for Mrs Maylie and Rose. After breakfast he had lessons with an old man in the village and in the afternoons he went for walks with Rose. In the evenings he did his homework and listened while Rose read aloud from a book or played the piano and sang. Three months passed in this way and life was perfect for Oliver again.

One beautiful hot summer afternoon, Oliver and Rose went for a very long walk. When they came back much later than usual, Rose sat down at the piano and began to play a sad tune. Suddenly she stopped playing and looked very pale.

Mrs Maylie got up quickly and put her arms round Rose.

"My dear girl, what's the matter?"

"I didn't want to worry you, Aunt, but I'm afraid I'm ill."

"You must go to bed now and if you're not better in the morning, I'll send for Dr Losberne."

"I'm sure I'll be well again in the morning, Aunt. Goodnight. Goodnight, Oliver."

But in the morning, Rose was worse. Mrs Maylie called Oliver and gave him two letters. One for Dr Losberne and one for her son, Harry, who loved Rose.

"Oliver, take these letters to the village inn and ask them to send them at once."

"I'll run there and back as fast as I can, Mrs Maylie!"

Oliver ran all the way to the village inn, and asked the innkeeper to send the letters straight away. As he was running out of the inn yard, he bumped into a tall man wearing a black cloak.

"Oh, I'm sorry, sir, I didn't see you. I hope I didn't hurt you?"

The man stared at Oliver. He seemed to recognise the boy.

"You young devil! What are you doing here?"

He shook his fist and took a step towards Oliver, then suddenly fell to the ground in a fit and started shaking. Oliver called for help for the mysterious stranger, then ran home as fast as he could. He was puzzled and frightened by the man's strange behaviour, but as soon as he was back with the Maylies he forgot all about it, because Rose was much worse.

The next day Dr Losberne and Harry Maylie arrived. While the doctor was with Rose, Harry spoke to his mother.

"Mother, you know I love Rose and want to marry her. When she is well, may I ask her to marry me?"

"Yes, of course! You know I love you both and if you get married, I'll be very happy. Ask her when she's well again."

Just then Dr Losberne came in. Mrs Maylie and Harry looked at him anxiously, and waited for him to speak.

"The danger is past. She will get well."

Rose grew stronger every day and a cheerful atmosphere returned to the cottage. Oliver went to his lessons every day and studied hard. Then he walked in the countryside with Harry and showed him where to find the most beautiful flowers for Rose. The days passed quickly.

One evening, Oliver was doing his homework. It was a hot day and he was sleepy. He finished the last exercise, closed his books and looked out into the garden. There, outside the window, looking at him, were two men—Fagin and the mysterious stranger!

"Help!" shouted Oliver. He jumped back from the window, and the men ran away. By the time Harry and Dr Losberne came out, there was no sign of them. The servants searched the fields around the house but they found no one. The next day Harry went to the village to ask about the strangers. But nobody knew anything.

"Oliver, my boy, maybe you were just tired and imagined those strangers," said Dr Losberne at last.

The incident was soon forgotten.

A few days later Rose was well enough to get up. It was a warm day and everyone was in the garden. Mrs Maylie was sewing and Harry and Rose were sitting under a tree, reading a book together. Suddenly, Harry put down the book.

"Rose, I want to speak to you. I think you know I love you. Will you marry me? I've already spoken to my mother and she agrees to our marriage if that's what you want, too."

"Harry, I can't marry you. You know I was a poor orphan when your mother took me in. You want to be a great politician. I'm afraid that if you marry me, your career will suffer."

"But Rose … you are more important to me than my career!"

"You say that now, but if you marry me, maybe one day you will regret it."

Harry was upset and decided to leave the next day with Dr Losberne. A few days later Mrs Maylie and Rose decided to take Oliver to the coast, on holiday. On their way, they stopped in London for three days. Oliver hoped that he would not meet anyone from Fagin's gang while he was there.

The Plot Against Oliver

*B*ack in the town where Oliver was born, Mr Bumble was now Master of the workhouse. Around the time of Rose's illness, he got married to the Mistress of the workhouse but it was not a happy marriage. He soon discovered that his wife had a strong character and she refused to obey him.

One day they had a big argument and Mr Bumble went out for a walk to calm down. While he was out it began to rain, so he went into an inn. It was empty—except for a tall man in a black cloak. The man looked at Mr Bumble for a while and then he spoke.

"You're Mr Bumble, an officer at the workhouse, aren't you?"

"I'm **Master** of the workhouse now!"

"You can help me, then," said the stranger, and he pushed a gold coin across the table to Mr Bumble. "About twelve years ago a boy called Oliver was born there."

"Oh, yes, Oliver Twist. I remember him."

"Was anybody with Oliver's mother when he was born?"

"Yes, Old Sally. She died last winter. But my wife was with her when she died and …"

Mr Bumble picked up the gold coin and looked at the stranger. The stranger pushed another coin across the table. Mr Bumble picked that up, too.

"Before Sally died, she told my wife a secret about Oliver and gave something to her."

"My name is Monks. Here's my address. I want to talk to your wife. Bring her to my house tomorrow night at 9 o'clock with the things Sally gave her. I'll pay you well."

The following night Mr and Mrs Bumble went to visit Monks at his house near the river. They gave him the locket and ring and he gave them twenty-five gold coins. As soon as they left, Monks opened the window and threw the things into the river.

"There! Now my secret is safe. No one can prove that Oliver Twist is my half-brother!"

The day after Oliver arrived in London, Nancy went to Fagin's house. She wanted some money to buy food for Bill, who was sick in bed. Just before she left, Monks came in. Nancy said goodnight and went out, but as she was closing the door she heard Oliver's name. She stood in the dark outside the door, held her breath and listened. She could hear Monks speaking.

"Oliver Twist is back in London. He's staying at the Park Hotel with an old woman and a young girl—the Maylies. I want to bring him back here. Together we'll make him a thief and see him hang, or if I can, I'll kill him myself! Then I'll get all our father's money. If you help me, I'll give you a share of the money."

When she heard this, Nancy wanted to help Oliver. She crept silently down the stairs and out into the street, then ran as fast as she could to the Park Hotel. There, she asked to speak to Miss Maylie, and was taken up to her room.

Rose was surprised to see Nancy, but she spoke to her kindly.

"Do I know you? Are you in trouble? Can I help you?"

"You don't know me, Miss, but I've got something important to tell you about Oliver. He's got a half-brother called Monks, who's a very bad man. Tonight I heard him talking. Monks knows Oliver's here in London and he's planning to kidnap him to make him a thief, or even worse—to kill him if he can!"

"Oh, poor Oliver! What am I going to do?"

"Is there anyone you trust, who can help you?"

"I think so … but where can I find you again … if I need to talk to you, or if you have anything else to tell me?"

"I'll walk on London Bridge every Sunday night between 11 and 12 o'clock—if I'm still alive. I've risked my life tonight to come and tell you this, but I wanted to help Oliver. Now I must go quickly before anyone finds out I've been here."

"Dear girl, why do you have to go back to these people? I can help you start a new life!" cried Rose.

"I must go back, because I love my husband—even though he's a bad man. I can't leave him."

"Thank you for coming to me. At least, let me give you some money."

"No, not a penny, sweet lady. Now I must go. Goodnight."

Rose stayed up all night thinking. Who could help her to save Oliver?

Nancy's Sacrifice

The next morning Rose was sitting at her desk trying to decide whether to ask Harry Maylie or Dr Losberne to help her. Her problem was solved when Oliver ran into the room with a big smile on his face.

"Rose, Mr Brownlow's in London! I've got his address. Can we go and see him?"

"Of course! Mr Brownlow has helped Oliver before! I'm sure he'll know what to do," thought Rose. She stood up and smiled at Oliver.

"What wonderful news! We'll go at once!"

Soon Rose and Oliver arrived at Mr Brownlow's house. The old man was delighted to see Oliver again, and listened as Oliver told him why he didn't come back with the books. Mrs Bedwin cried tears of joy and even Mr Grimwig was pleased. Rose asked to speak to Mr Brownlow in private. She told him about her conversation with Nancy and the kind old man agreed to help her find Monks and make him share his father's money with Oliver.

On Sunday night Fagin was at Bill Sikes' house. At 11 o'clock Nancy got ready to go out.

"Where are you going?"

"I don't feel very well, Bill. I want some fresh air."

"Then put your head out of the window."

"No, I want to go for a walk outside. I've been in the house all day."

Bill locked the door and put the key in his pocket.

"Now sit down. You're not going anywhere, my girl."

"Bill, let me go, just for one hour!"

Nancy was angry now. She began to shout and scream, and fought with Bill, trying to get the key, but it was no use. The fight went on for an hour, and then they heard the clock striking midnight. When she heard the sound, Nancy suddenly calmed down. She sat down on a chair and tears rolled down her pale face, but a few moments later she began to laugh. The two men looked at each other in surprise.

"What a strange girl she is!"

"Take no notice of her, Bill. She'll be all right in a few minutes."

Fagin said goodnight and got up to leave. As he walked home he thought about Nancy's strange behaviour.

"I think Nancy's got a secret. Why did she want to go out tonight? Was she going to meet someone? I must find out where she goes and who she talks to. I'll tell one of my boys to follow her."

The following Sunday Bill was not at home. At 11 o'clock Nancy put on her hat and coat and went out. She looked up and down the street and when she was sure it was empty, set off quickly towards London Bridge. She didn't notice a boy, standing in a doorway, but he saw her and followed her silently, keeping in the shadows.

It was a cold, dark night and few people were out. When Nancy reached London Bridge, she saw a carriage waiting at the side of the road. Inside were Rose and Mr Brownlow. Nancy told them where they could find Monks, and then began to describe him. She didn't notice the boy who was hiding behind the carriage listening to every word she said.

"He's a tall, strong man. He's got dark hair and very deep-set eyes. He must be about twenty-six but he looks much older. On his neck is ..."

"A red mark, like a burn?" cried Mr Brownlow.

"Yes! Do you know him?"

"I think I do."

"Thank you for helping us," said Rose. "But please let us help you. Tell us the names of the thieves. Then the police will catch them all. We can give you some money and help you to start a new, honest life."

Nancy shook her head.

"I can't betray the man I love. I've told you where to find Monks because I want to help Oliver, but I can't tell you any more. I don't know why, but I feel afraid tonight, and I want to get home quickly before anyone sees me here."

Later that night Fagin sat in his cold room looking at the boy who was asleep on the floor. Fagin's face was pale and his eyes were red. He was biting his black nails and waiting for Bill Sikes. At last he heard heavy footsteps on the stairs. Bill came in, sat down and put a bag on the table.

"It was a difficult job, but we managed it at last."

Then he noticed Fagin's expression.

"What's wrong?"

"Nancy's betrayed us! If you don't believe me, ask that boy! He followed her tonight and ..."

"What?"

Bill shook the sleeping boy and listened to his story.

"Nancy! I'll kill her for this!"

Before Fagin could stop him, Bill ran out of the house, cursing and swearing.

Chapter 9

Nancy was asleep when Bill got home.

"Get up!"

"Bill, what is it? Why are you looking at me like that?"

"You know very well. Where were you tonight? What did you do?"

He threw her across the room and picked up a heavy wooden stick. Nancy ran to him and held his arm.

"Bill, don't hurt me! We can go away and start a new life …"

Bill pushed her away from him, looked once into her eyes, then raised the stick and hit her on the head with all his strength.

When the sun came up, Nancy was lying dead on the floor in a pool of blood. Bill lit a fire and burnt the stick, then tried to clean the blood off his clothes. Finally he went out, locking the door behind him, and walked quickly away from the house.

Justice is Served

T he next day the news of Nancy's murder was in all the newspapers. Everyone in London was talking about it, and everyone wanted the murderer to be caught. Mr Brownlow and Rose read the news too, and felt very sad.

"Poor Nancy," said Rose, with tears in her eyes, "She died because she wanted to help Oliver."

"As soon as we have found Monks we must look for Nancy's murderer."

They decided to send for Dr Losberne and Harry Maylie, the two men they knew they could trust to help them. The doctor and Harry arrived that afternoon and late in the evening they brought Monks to Mr Brownlow's house. They took him to Mr Brownlow's study and left the two men together. Monks was angry.

"You were my father's oldest friend! Why have you brought me here like a criminal?"

"It's because of my friendship for your father that I brought you here, Edward Leeford. Yes, of course I know your real name! I know many other things too—about the gangs you belonged to and the trouble you have been in abroad. And don't forget I was going to marry your father's sister, but she died. I know the sad story of your father's marriages, too. After his first wife—your mother—died, he met a young woman and fell in love. Soon after this marriage he had to go abroad suddenly, but before he left he gave me a picture of this girl and asked me to take care of her if anything happened to him. I still have the picture and that's how I recognised Oliver. He looks exactly like his mother.

Well, while your father was abroad, he got ill and died. When his wife heard the news, she was so upset she ran away. I couldn't find her and so Oliver was born in the workhouse. Your father left his money to you and your half-brother, Oliver. I want to make sure you share the money with him."

"You can't prove that Oliver is my half-brother!"

"Ah, but I can! I have spoken to Mr Bumble who is Master of the workhouse where Oliver was born. He told me about the locket and ring. You can choose. Sign these papers to say that you will share your father's money with Oliver or I will tell the police everything I know about you!"

"I've got friends who can help me to hide from the police, or I can go abroad. Why should I sign those papers?"

"I know who your friends are—thieves and murderers. And maybe I know something that you don't. The police arrested Fagin and Jack Dawkins today. Soon they will catch all the other members of the gang, too. Then who will help you?"

Monks turned pale.

"If I call for the police now you will get a fair trial, but we both know you will go to prison."

Monks walked angrily up and down the room. At last he spoke.

"Very well, if I sign the papers, will I be free to go?"

"You have my word as a gentleman."

Monks was angry, but signed the papers and threw the pen down on the table. Then, with a curse, he walked out into the dark street. Mr Brownlow picked up the papers.

"Thanks to Nancy, Oliver is safe. And now we must hunt down her murderer ..."

When the police caught Fagin, Toby Crackit and Charley Bates were with him, but they escaped up the chimney. Later that evening they were hiding in an old house near the river in one of the dirtiest, poorest parts of the city. As they were looking out of a window, they suddenly saw a white dog, with blood on its fur and feet.

"Bill's dog! Bill must be somewhere near here!"

"If he comes here I won't help him," shouted Charley. "I'll call for the police."

A few minutes later, someone knocked at the door. Toby opened it and Bill Sikes ran in. He looked sick and tired and sat down in a chair with the dog at his feet.

"The police are after me with a crowd of people but they didn't see me come in here. Can I stay and hide till they've gone?"

"Monster! Murderer!" shouted Charley.

Outside in the street there was a big crowd of people and policemen. Charley opened the window and shouted loudly, "Help! Police! The murderer is here! ..."

Bill pulled him away from the window and knocked him to the floor. At that moment there was a loud knock at the door.

"This is the police! Open the door or we'll break it down!"

Bill looked out of the window.

"Toby, give me a rope and I'll climb out onto the roof and drop down into the river at the back of the house. They won't catch me!"

He climbed out of the window and tied one end of the rope round the chimney.

He was tying the other end round his chest when suddenly he gave a loud cry.

"Oh, no! The eyes! I can see Nancy's eyes! ..."

He fell off the roof and the rope slipped up and tightened round his neck. Bill Sikes was dead. The dog howled and tried to reach his master.

Fagin, that wicked old man with blood on his hands, had a fair trial, was found guilty and hanged. Monks escaped to America, soon spent all his money and returned to a life of crime. He eventually died in prison. Charley Bates decided an honest life was best, and found a good job on a farm.

Rose married Harry Maylie and Mrs Maylie went to live with them in a little house in the country. Mr Brownlow adopted Oliver and bought a house near their friends, the Maylies. When he told them the story of Oliver's parents, they all realised that Rose was in fact the sister of Oliver's mother, Agnes. So finally, Oliver found himself with a family he did not know he had and lived the rest of his life in happiness.

THE END

Activities

At the Workhouse

Read or listen to Chapter 1 and tick (✓) the boxes True or False.

	True	False
1 Old Sally had fifteen children.		
2 The young woman had a baby girl.		
3 There was some hair in the locket.		
4 The children at the workhouse loved Mr Bumble.		
5 The food at the workhouse was not very good.		

What do you think?

1 Why do you think Mr Bumble was angry with Oliver?
2 How is your life different from Oliver's life so far?
3 What do your parents do when you want more things?

Language Practice

1 *Look at the pictures and match them into pairs to make phrases from Chapter 1.*

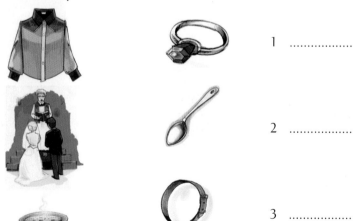

1 ....

2 ....

3 ....

11 *Read the rule and fill in the gaps with the correct word,* where, which *or* who.

We use:
- *who* when we talk about people,
- *which* when we talk about things and
- *where* when we talk about places.

1   Workhouses were special places .... poor people lived.
2   The young woman gave Sally a chain .... had a locket on it.
3   Mr Bumble was a man .... worked in the workhouse.
4   Sally was the old woman .... helped the doctor when Oliver was born.
5   The room .... Mr Bumble locked Oliver was cold and dark.
6   The soup .... the boys ate was mostly water.

What happens next?

Look at the scenes below. Which one do you think happens next in the story? Explain why.

Life with Mr Sowerberry

😊 Comprehension 🎧

Read or listen to Chapter 2 and put the following events in the correct chronological order.

a   Oliver ate the dog's food. ....

b   Someone kicked the door and shouted. ....

c   Mr Bumble took Oliver to Mr Sowerberry's shop. ....

d   Oliver stayed in the dark room for a week.   e.g. ...*1*....

e   Oliver decided to run away. ....

f   Mr Bumble saw Mr Sowerberry in the street. ....

g   Noah tried to make Oliver cry. ....

What do you think?

1   Why do you think Oliver was frightened of sleeping in the room with the coffins?

2   Are you frightened of anything? Why? Tell the class.

3   If you had to leave your house in a hurry, because of a fire, for example, what three things would you take with you? Describe each thing and say why it is important to you.

Language Practice

1   Fill in the gaps with the correct prepositions.

1   Mr Bumble met Mr Sowerberry .... the workhouse.

2   Mr Bumble and Mr Sowerberry went .... to make arrangements for Oliver to leave the workhouse.

3   The coffin was .... the table.

4   Oliver slept .... the shop counter.

II Read and circle the correct item.

1 Mr Bumble .... to the notice on the door.
   A bowed   B pointed   C tired

2 Oliver ate the dog's food ....
   A politely   B hardly   C hungrily

3 Mr Sowerberry was always .... to Oliver and so Noah got
   jealous.
   A kind   B tall   C horrible

4 Oliver stopped crying and .... his eyes.
   A pulled   B pinched   C wiped

5 Oliver packed some .... and left.
   A stairs   B socks   C shutters

Guess the meaning

*Read the following paragraph and guess the meaning of the
words/phrases that are printed in bold.*

A small dog lived in the street near my school. It was black with **dirt** and thin because it lived outside all the time and slept on the ground. But it was **cheerful** and ran up to me every day wagging its tail. Then I gave it a biscuit. One day, I **woke up** late and my father took me to school in the car, so that I didn't miss my first lesson. When it was lunch time, I **realised** that I forgot to give the dog a biscuit this morning. I went to the shop and **bought** some.

Now, you draw a picture for this short story in your notebook!

The little dog was waiting for me when I came out of the shop. When my friend saw the little dog, he wanted to take it home. Now the little dog has a new home and my friend has a lovely pet.

On the Streets of London

😊 Comprehension 🎧

Read or listen to Chapter 3 and answer the following questions.

Who …

1 … was very hungry and tired?   e.g. *Oliver*
2 … introduced Oliver to Fagin?   ....
3 … told Oliver about the handkerchiefs?   ....
4 … wanted to learn how to bring wallets home?   ....
5 … thought Oliver stole his handkerchief?   ....

What do you think?

1 Why do you think Jack helped Oliver?
2 Why do you think Mr Brownlow helped Oliver?
3 Why do you think Fagin played the game with the boys?
4 What did Oliver feel when he realised what kind of people Fagin and the boys were?

Language Practice

1 Join the two halves to make complete sentences.

1 I can't believe ….	… asleep as soon as I got home.
2 The boys ran …	… the cat caught the rat.
3 As quick as a flash, …	… like the wind.
4 I was so tired that I fell …	… my luck.

....
....
....
....

11 Use the words in the box to label the items in the picture.

| ceiling | rat | wall | doorstep | floor | wallet |
| mattress | corner | handkerchiefs | smoke | pan |

What happens next?

Look at the following pictures. Discuss how these things may be important in the next chapter.

books

coins

a portrait

new clothes

Oliver meets Mr Brownlow

 **Comprehension**

Read or listen to Chapter 4 and circle the correct answer.

1   The old lady was Mr Brownlow's ....
    A   wife   B   housekeeper   C   sister

2   Mr Brownlow stared at the picture because ....
    A   ... the lady's face was beautiful.
    B   ... the lady's eyes were sad.
    C   ... the lady looked just like Oliver.

3   Mr Brownlow was .... in his study when Oliver came in.
    A   reading   B   eating   C   writing

4   Mr Grimwig didn't like ....
    A   old men   B   boys   C   books

5   Mr Brownlow wanted Oliver to bring back some ....
    A   money   B   books and money   C   books

What do you think?

1   Why did Mr Grimwig want Oliver to go out for Mr Brownlow?
2   What do you think has happened to Oliver?
3   What qualities do you look for in a friend?

Language Practice

1   Underline the correct word.

1   The dog won't bite if you **stroke / knock** it gently.
2   It is very **pleasant / comfortable** to sit outside in the sun.
3   When we heard the good news, we all smiled **happily / really**.
4   I'm so happy here. Please don't ever **laugh at me / send me away**.
5   Please **change / comb** your clothes before you go out.

II Match the words with the pictures to make phrases from Chapter 4. Then use these phrases to make up a story.

1 sitting ....

2 young ....

3 new ....

4 good ....

Read the following paragraph and guess the meaning of the words/phrases that are printed in bold.

Last night I watched a police movie. A thief with a **pistol** went into a bank and stole money. When a man pressed the alarm, the **criminal** shot him. The **bullet** hit the man in the arm and he fell down, covered in **blood**. Then the police arrived and went in carefully. They **raised** their guns in front of their faces and told the thief to put down his gun. Luckily the injured man did not die, so the thief was not a **murderer**, too.

Kidnapped

 **Comprehension**

Read or listen to Chapter 5, then complete these sentences.

1 When the boys went home without Oliver, Fagin was very
   ....
2 Fagin was afraid that Oliver might go to the ....
3 Nancy put on a clean .... and pretended to cry.
4 Nancy threw Fagin's .... into the fire.
5 Bill loaded his .... and put it on the table.

What do you think?

1 Why do you think the boys stayed with Fagin?
2 What do you think Fagin thought of Bill Sikes?
3 What is the most frightening story you have read or heard?

Language Practice

1 *Use the words/phrases in the box to describe these characters.*

| tall   old   thin   long curly hair   well-built |
| about 35   young   greasy hair   rosy cheeks |

II Fill in the gaps with the correct expression from the box.

cheered up	ashamed	going on	too much	no use

1 What's .... in here?
2 When I failed the test, it was .... for me and I cried.
3 We all .... when we heard the good news.
4 That was a terrible thing to do. Aren't you .... ?
5 We tried to get over the wall, but it was .... It was too high.

What happens next?

Read the three ideas below and guess which one happens next. Choose one and write notes to continue the story in the space below.

Oliver runs away from Bill

Nancy tells the police about Oliver

Oliver gets hurt during the robbery

The Robbery

 Comprehension

Read or listen to Chapter 6 and answer the following questions.

1 Who went with Oliver to rob the big house?
2 What happened to Oliver when he got inside the house?
3 How did Oliver get under the tree?
4 What happened to Oliver when the servants found him the next morning?
5 Why were the Maylies surprised when they saw Oliver?

What do you think?

1 How do you think Mr Giles felt when he realised he had shot a little boy?
2 What do you think Bill Sikes and Toby Crackit did after they left Oliver?
3 Has anyone ever asked you to do something you knew was wrong? What did you do?

Language Practice

1 What's the word? The jumbled words below are from Chapter 6. Find them and write them down.

1 Someone who is not brave.   *drawoc* = ...
2 A child who has no parents.   *prahon* = ...
3 Your father's sister.   *tuna* = ...
4 You bend these to sit down.   *sneek* = ...
5 Somewhere to keep things.   *mosterroo* = ...

11 *Draw a line to match the words with their pictures. Then use these words to make up a story.*

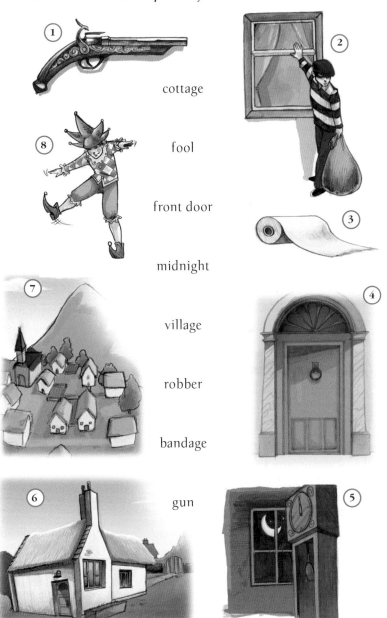

cottage

fool

front door

midnight

village

robber

bandage

gun

83

A Home for Oliver

 **Comprehension**

Read or listen to Chapter 7 and correct the mistakes.

1 One beautiful dry summer afternoon, Oliver and Rose went for a very long walk.
2 Mrs Maylie got up quickly and put her arms round Oliver.
3 "Oliver, take these letters to the village inn and ask them to send them tomorrow."
4 Oliver called for help for the mysterious stranger, then walked home as fast as he could.
5 He finished the last letter, closed his books and looked out into the garden.
6 "I'm afraid that if you marry me, your mother will suffer."

1 .... = ...   4 .... = ...
2 .... = ...   5 .... = ...
3 .... = ...   6 .... = ...

What do you think?

1 What do you think Fagin and the mysterious stranger were doing in the garden?
2 What do you do if someone is ill? How does that compare with what they did in the 1800's?
3 How do you spend your school holidays?

Language Practice

1 *Many long English words are made from shorter words. Read these short words and find the longer words from Chapter 7.*

1 mystery...........................   4 inn ....
2 behave ....   5 marry ....
3 peace...........................   6 politics...........................

84

II *Match the phrasal verbs below to their meanings and pictures.*
Then write the three missing definitions and draw the three
missing pictures.

1	take sb in	a	To shout because you are in pain.		i
	d ⇌ ii				
2	cheer up	b	....		ii
	⇌				
3	get up	c	To lift sth using your fingers.		iii
	⇌				
4	fall down	d	To let sb stay in your house.		iv
	⇌				
5	cry out	e	....		v
	⇌				
6	pick up	f	To do sth more quickly.		vi
	⇌				
7	set off	g	To fall to the ground.		vii
	⇌				
8	put on	h	....		viii
	⇌				
9	hurry up	i	To start to go somewhere		ix
	⇌				

85

The Plot Against Oliver

 *Comprehension*

Read or listen to Chapter 8 and tick the correct box.

1 Mr Bumble was now .... of the workhouse.

master	
officer	
mistress	

2 The stranger gave Mr Bumble a gold

locket.	
ring.	
coin.	

3 Monks threw the things into the

river.	
street.	
safe.	

4 Nancy went to speak to

Rose Maylie.	
Mr Brownlow.	
Monks.	

5 Nancy walked on London Bridge every

Friday.	
Saturday.	
Sunday.	

What do you think?

1 Who do you think could help Rose?
2 What would you do if you were in Rose's place?
3 What is the bravest thing you have ever done?

1 Fill in the crossword and discover the relationship between Oliver and Monks.

1   Nancy held her .... and listened.
2   The opposite of dead is ....
3   Mr Bumble went for a walk to .... down.
4   The name of the old man who taught the boys how to steal was ....
5   Mrs Bumble refused to .... her husband.
6   Monks' house was near the ....
7   A round, flat, metal object used as money is a ....
8   When you have a .... you don't want to tell anyone.
9   Mr Bumble is Mrs Bumble's ....
10 Nancy walked on London .... on Sunday night between 11 o' clock and midnight.
11 When you give somebody your .... , you tell them where you live.
12 When you have an .... you call the doctor.

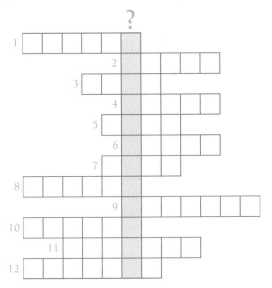

Nancy's Sacrifice

 *Comprehension*

Read or listen to Chapter 9, then fill in the gaps of the summary below with one of the names from the box. There is an extra name that you don't need.

Bill	Mr Brownlow	Monks	Oliver
Nancy	Rose	Fagin	

Rose and Oliver went to see (1) .... He agreed to help Rose find Monks.

On Sunday night Nancy wanted to go out but Bill didn't let her. (2) .... thought Nancy had a secret. The next Sunday Bill wasn't at home so (3) .... went out at eleven o' clock. She didn't notice that a boy was following her. On London Bridge she met (4) .... and Mr Brownlow. She described (5) .... and told them where to find him. The boy heard everything and ran home to tell Fagin.

Later that night, (6) .... was so angry that he ran home and killed Nancy with a big stick.

What do you think?

1   What sort of person do you think Nancy was?

2   Why do you think Rose didn't ask her aunt to help her and asked a stranger, Mr Brownlow?

3   Think of a time when you helped or wanted to help someone. What happened?

Language Practice

I   Use the correct word from the box to fill in the gaps in the following sentences.

| cried | rolled | burnt | solved | biting | keeping |

1   Rose .... her problem with Mr Brownlow's help.
2   When Mrs Bedwin saw Oliver again, she .... tears of joy.
3   When Nancy heard the clock strike midnight, tears ....
    down her face.
4   The boy who followed Nancy was .... in the shadows.
5   Fagin was .... his nails as he was waiting for Bill.
6   Bill .... the stick before he left the house.

II   Imagine that the story ends differently. Write a paragraph with your ending starting with Nancy's words: "Bill, don't hurt me. We can go away and start a new life …".

III   Imagine that you have noticed someone following you for the past few days. Write a description of your imaginary character.

Justice is Served

 *Comprehension*

Read or listen to Chapter 10 and answer the questions.

1   What was Monks' real name?
2   What happened to Oliver's real father?
3   How did Toby and Charley know that Bill Sikes was nearby?
4   How did Bill plan to escape from the police?
5   What was the relationship between Rose and Oliver's mother?

What do you think?

1   If Oliver Twist's story continued, what do you think he would do when he grew up?
2   Do you like the end of the story? Would you like to change anything in the story?
3   Why do you think Bill Sikes became a criminal?

Language Practice

1   Use the words and phrases in the box to complete the paragraph about a murder.

arrested	broke down	fair trial	free
guilty	rest of his life	newspapers	fur

Last week there was a terrible story in the (1) .... It was about the death of a young woman. The murderer escaped but the police found him because they saw his dog, with blood on its (2) .... , sitting outside an old house. They (3) .... the door of the house and (4) .... the man. He will have a (5) .... and if he is innocent he will be set (6) .... If he is found (7) .... he will go to prison. Some people say that, if he is the murderer, he should stay in prison for the (8) ....

What's the moral?

A moral is a lesson about what is right or wrong, that you can learn from a story. What do you think the moral is in "Oliver Twist"? Choose one from those listed below or make up your own.

- You should always protect those you love.
- Crime does not pay.
- You always get what you deserve in the end.
- Money is not the most important thing in life.
- Always try to help people.
- You can not run away from your problems.
- You don't need to be strong to win.
- Families should stick together.
- Your own: ....

Family Trees

I   Look at Oliver's family tree. Put the names of the people in the right place to find out what Oliver's real family name was.

| Mr Leeford | Oliver | Monks | Agnes | Monk's mother |

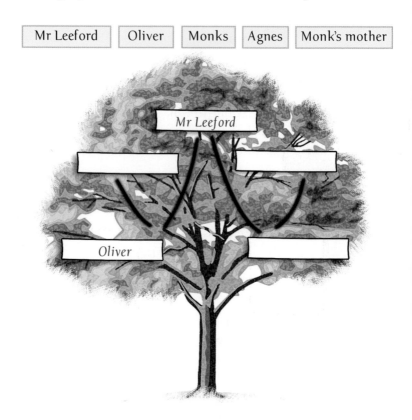

Oliver's real name is not 'Twist' . It is Oliver ....

II   Now draw you own family tree. Write the names of your parents and your grandparents. You may need to ask your parents for information. If you have brothers or sisters, add their names in the boxes next to yours. You may add more boxes if you need to.

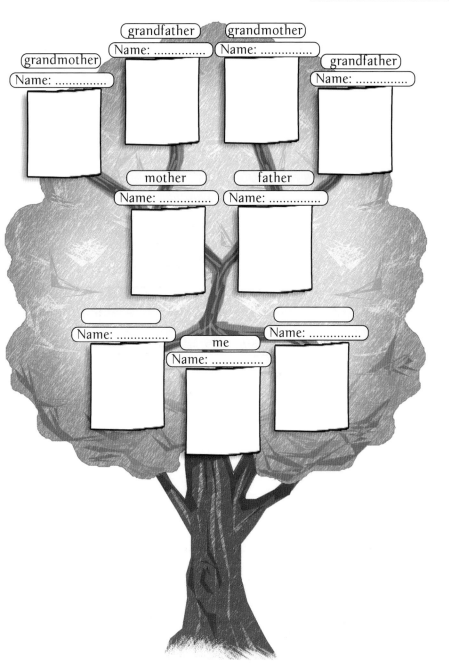

93

Child Workers

I   Look at the kind of jobs children did in Victorian England.

What do you think these children are doing?

a   In picture 1?
b   In picture 2?
c   In picture 3?
d   In picture 4?

II   Do you think it was right for children to do this kind of work?

III   Why do you think children did these jobs?

IV   Which job do you think was the worst/most dangerous/the best?

V *Read the following article which describes life for poor people in Victorian London.*

Life in the Workhouses

I went into London last week and noticed that many poor men and women lived in workhouses. Their children lived in other workhouses away from their parents. Nobody really cares about them there.

I know that workhouses are there to help poor people. They have no money or family to take care of them.

When the children leave the workhouses, they do not know what it is like to have a family. They meet criminals and get involved in crime.

I think that families should not be split up when they go into the workhouses.

Charles Dickens wrote many articles on the terrible way poor people, especially children, lived in Victorian England. Write a similar article, based on child workers, using the answers and information from the exercises on the opposite page. Use this plan to help you.

Plan – Writing an Article

Paragraph 1 –What is happening at the moment.
Paragraph 2 – The reasons it is happening.
Paragraph 3 – The effects it has on the children.
Paragraph 4 – The possible solutions.

Word List

Look these words/phrases up in the dictionary and fill in their meanings.

Chapter 1

a long way (phr) ....

a piece of bread (phr) ....

alone (adj) ....

another (det) ....

appear (v) ....

arrive (n) ....

as usual (phr) ....

at last (phr) ....

be afraid (phr) ....

be born (phr) ....

be on one's way (phr) ....

beat (beat – beaten) (v) ....

become (became – become) (v) ....

birth (n) ....

by the fire (phr) ....

cannot believe one's ears (exp) ....

cellar (n) ....

chain (n) ....

choose (chose – chosen) (v) ....

collar (n) ....

come (came – come) (v) ....

could (modal v) ....

cradle (n) ....

cry out (phr v) ....

dead (adj) ....

decide (v) ....

die (v) ....

during (prep) ....

elbow (n) ....

empty (adj) ....

enough (pron) ....

especially (adv) ....

fall back (v) ....

fall down (fell – fallen) (phr v) ....

fear (n) ....

find (found – found) (v) ....

frightened (adj) ....

get (got – got) (v) ....

give (gave – given) (v) ....

gloves (n, pl) ....

Go on! (exp) ....

go red (phr) ....

gold (adj) ....

hard (adj) ....

have a bad temper (phr) ....

hear (heard – heard) (v) ....

hit (hit – hit) (v) ....

hold out (held – held) (v) ....

hope (n) ....

hopefully (adv) ....

hungry (adj) ....

keep sth for oneself (phr) ....

keep sth safe (phr) ....

kind (adj) ....

kindly (adv) ....

know (knew – known) (v) ....

late (adj) ....

let (let – let) (v) ....

lick (v) ....

lie (lay – lain) (v) ....

life (n) ....

lock (v) ....

locket (n) ....

locks of hair (phr) ....

look after (phr v) ....

manage (v) ....

master (n) ....

notice (n) ....

nowhere else (phr) ....

only (adv) ....

pain (n) ....

pale (adj) ....

pay (paid – paid) (v) ....

pick up (v) ....

pillow (n) ....

pocket (n) ....

poor (adj) ....

possible (adj) ....

pot (n) ....

pregnant (adj) ....

push (v) ....

put on (put – put) (phr v) ....

receive (v) ....

rest (v) ....

serve (v) ....

shake (shook – shaken) (v) ....

shout (v) ....

sick (adj) ....

sigh (v) ....

silence (n) ....

sit up (sat – sat) (phr v) ....

slowly (adv) ....

soon (adv) ....

spoon (n) ....

stick (n) ....

strange (adj) ....

strength (n) ....

strict (adj) ....

suddenly (adv) ....

surname (n) ....

take care of sb (phr) ....

take off (took – taken) (phr v) ....

take sb (to a place) (phr) ....

think (thought – thought) (v) ....

trouble (v) ....

ungrateful (adj) ....

uniform (n) ....

until (conj) ....

useful (adj) ....

wear (wore – worn) (v) ....

wedding ring (n) ....

whisper (v) ....

workhouse (n) ....

worn out (adj) ....

Chapter 2

against the wall (phr) ....

agree (v) ....

arrangement (n) ....

as soon as (phr-conj) ....

bad (worse – worst) (adj) ....

be nasty to sb (phr) ....

because of (phr-prep) ....

bow (v) ....

burst into tears (phr) ....

call sb (v) ....

candle (n) ....

cap (n) ....

chat (v) ....

clothes (n, pl) ....

coal cellar (n) ....

coffin (n) ....

coffin maker (n) ....

continue (v) ....

downstairs (adv) ....

enjoy (v) ....

finished (adj) ....

follow (v) ....

fox (n) ....

get jealous (phr) ....

gloomy (adj) ....

grow (grew – grown) (v) ....

handkerchief (n) ....

hardly (adv) ....

hide (hid – hidden) (v) ....

horrible (adj) ....

hungrily (adv) ....

hurry up (phr v) ....

idea (n) ....

kick (v) ....

laugh (v) ....

leave sb (left – left) (v) ....

look like (v) ....

make one's life difficult (exp) ....

meat (n) ....

murder (v) ....

notice (v) ....

own (v) ....

penny (n, pl: pence) ....

pinch (v) ....

point to (v) ....

politely (adv) ....

pull (v) ....

quietly (adv) ....

run away (ran – run) (phr v) ....

send (sent – sent) (v) ....

servant girl (n) ....

set off (set – set) (phr v) ....

shop counter (n) ....

shutters (n, pl) ....

smile at sb (phr) ....

so far (phr) ....

socks (n, pl) ....

stairs (n, pl) ....

stand (stood – stood) (v) ....

stay (v) ....

supper (n) ....

tall (adj) ....

taste (v) ....

tear (n) ....

through (prep) ....

tie up (phr v) ....

unlock (v) ....

walk past (phr) ....

watch (v) ....

wife (n) ....

wipe (v) ....

wood (n) ....

you little bag of bones (exp) ....

Chapter 3

admire (v) ....

area (n) ....

artful (adj) ....

at once (phr) ....

be on the road (phr) ....

bleed (bled – bled) (v) ....

bookshop (n) ....

buy (bought – bought) (v) ....

cannot believe one's luck (exp) ....

carefully (adv) ....

carriage (n) ....

ceiling (n) ....

check (v) ....

cheerful (adj) ....

colourful (adj) ....

corner (n) ....

crowd (n) ....

curiously (adv) ....

dirt (n) ....

disappear (v) ....

dodger (n) ....

doorstep (n) ....

explain (v) ....

fall asleep (phr) ....

feel (felt – felt) (v) ....

fork (n) ....

friendly (adj) ....

gentleman (n, pl: gentlemen) ....

gratefully (adv) ....

greasy (adj) ....

ground (n) ....

hang (hung – hung) (v) ....

He'll do! (exp) ....

ill (adj) ....

innocent (adj) ....

line (n) ....

loudly (adv) ....

mattress (n) ....

Meet my friend! (exp) ....

pan (n) ....

perfect (adj) ....

playfully (adv) ....

pleased (adj) ....

quick as a flash (phr) ....

rat (n) ....

reach (v) ....

realise (v) ....

remember (v) ....

run like the wind (exp) ....

secretly (adv) ....

seem (v) ....

show (showed – showed) (v) ....

silk (adj) ....

slip (v) ....

smoke (n) ....

stall (n) ....

stare at (v) ....

Word List

steal (stole – stolen) (v) ....

suppose (v) ....

teach (taught – taught) (v) ....

terrified (adj) ....

thief (n, pl: thieves) ....

top hat (n) ....

towards (prep) ....

turn (v) ....

understand (understood – understood) (v) ....

voice (n) ....

wake up (woke – woken) (phr v) ....

wallet (n) ....

wash (v) ....

well-made (adj) ....

What's the matter? (exp) ....

whole (adj) ....

win (won – won) (v) ....

winner (n) ....

wonder (v) ....

Chapter 4

a pack of lies (phr) ....

above (prep) ....

below (prep) ....

bring (brought – brought) (v) ....

change (n) ....

change (v) ....

comb (v) ....

comfortable (adj) ....

cool (adj) ....

exactly (adv) ....

fill with (v) ....

gaslight (n) ....

get up (phr v) ....

happily (adv) ....

housekeeper (n) ....

it grew dark (phr) ....

knock (n) ....

knock at (v) ....

laugh at sb (phr) ....

light (lit – lit) (v) ....

move (v) ....

must (modal v) ....

opposite (prep) ....

..., or I'll eat my hat! (exp) ....

out of the corner of one's eyes (phr) ....

pass (v) ....

pleasant (adj) ....

put one's head on one side (phr) ....

really (adv) ....

send sb away (phr) ....

seriously (adv) ....

shilling (n) ....

side (n) ....

sitting room (n) ....

straight back (phr) ....

stroke (v) ....

study (n) ....

trust (v) ....

truth (n) ....

Chapter 5

apron (n) ....

bar (n) ....

be ashamed (phr) ....

blood (n) ....

bonnet (n) ....

bullet (n) ....

by the time (phr) ....

care (v) ....

cheek (n) ....

cheer up (phr v) ....

criminal (n) ....

curly (adj) ....

dangerous (adj) ....

dirty (adj) ....

drag sb/sth (v) ....

escape (v) ....

find out (found – found) (phr v) ....

following (adj) ....

forward (adv) ....

grab (v) ....

growl (v) ....

gun-powder (n) ....

hold (v) ....

hurt (hurt – hurt) (v) ....

it's no use (exp) ....

kidnap (v) ....

kill (v) ....

load (v) ....

loaded (adj) ....

lose (lost – lost) (v) ....

murderer (n) ....

noise (n) ....

pistol (n) ....

police station (n) ....

pretend (v) ....

push sb away (phr) ....

raise (v) ....

rob (v) ....

rosy (adj) ....

rush (v) ....

scared (adj) ....

serious (adj) ....

snatch (v) ....

sooner or later (phr) ....

stolen (adj) ....

straw (adj) ....

stupid (adj) ....

terrible (adj) ....

This was too much. (exp) ....

throw (threw – thrown) (v) ....

tightly (adv) ....

well-built (adj) ....

What's going on in here? (exp) ....

worried (adj) ....

You young devil! (exp) ....

Chapter 6

already (adv) ....

asleep (adj) ....

aunt (n) ....

badly (adv) ....

bandage (n) ....

bang (n) ....

bitter cold (phr) ....

cottage (n) ....

covered in (phr) ....

coward (n) ....

cry (n) ....

darkness (n) ....

difficulty (n) ....

drop (v) ....

expect (v) ....

faint (v) ....

fall down on one's knees (phr) ....

fetch (v) ....

finally (adv) ....

flash of light (phr) ....

foggy (adj) ....

fool (n) ....

front door (n) ....

gasp (v) ....

gun (n) ....

in surprise (phr) ....

in the distance (phr) ....

instead of (phr-prep) ....

lift (v) ....

lonely (adj) ....

make noise (phr) ....

midnight (n) ....

orphan (n) ....

pull out (a gun) (phr) ....

robber (n) ....

robbery (n) ....

ruined (adj) ....

shoot (shot – shot) (v) ....

should (modal v) ....

silently (adv) ....

sleep (n) ....

stagger (v) ....

storeroom door (n) ....

surely (adv) ....

take a step (phr) ....

take sb in (phr v) ....

the country (n) ....

travel (v) ....

upstairs (adv) ....

village (n) ....

weak (adj) ....

Chapter 7

anxiously (adv) ....

atmosphere (n) ....

behaviour (n) ....

bump into (v) ....

call for help (phr) ....

career (n) ....

cloak (n) ....

Word List

coast (n) ....

countryside (n) ....

fist (n) ....

forget (forgot – forgotten) (v) ....

gang (n) ....

garden (n) ....

great (adj) ....

imagine (v) ....

in a fit (phr) ....

incident (n) ....

inn (n) ....

innkeeper (n) ....

marriage (n) ....

marry (v) ....

may (modal v) ....

mysterious (adj) ....

no sign of (phr) ....

peaceful (adj) ....

pick flowers (phr) ....

politician (n) ....

put one's arms around sb (phr) ....

puzzled (adj) ....

read aloud (phr) ....

recognise (v) ....

regret (v) ....

return (v) ....

search (v) ....

send for (phr v) ....

sew (sewed – sewn) (v) ....

sing (sang – sung) (v) ....

sleepy (adj) ....

son (n) ....

straight away (adv) ....

stranger (n) ....

suffer (v) ....

The danger is past. (exp) ....

tune (n) ....

walk (n) ....

yard (n) ....

Chapter 8

address (n) ....

alive (adj) ....

argument (n) ....

at least (phr) ....

be in trouble (phr) ....

bridge (n) ....

calm down (phr v) ....

character (n) ....

coin (n) ....

creep (crept – crept) (v) ....

discover (v) ....

even though (phr-conj) ....

except for (phr-prep) ....

half-brother (n) ....

hang (hanged – hanged) (v) ....

hold one's breath (phr) ....

husband (n) ....

illness (n) ....

mistress (n) ....

obey (v) ....

officer (n) ....

plan (v) ....

plot (n) ....

prove (proved – proven) (v) ....

refuse (v) ....

risk (v) ....

river (n) ....

safe (adj) ....

secret (n) ....

share (n) ....

stay up (phr v) ....

surprised (adj) ....

Chapter 9

betray (v) ....

bite (bit – bitten) (v) ....

burn (burnt – burnt) (v) ....

burn (n) ....

catch (caught – caught) (v) ....

conversation (n) ....

cry tears of joy (phr) ....

curse (v) ....

deep-set (adj) ....

delighted (adj) ....

describe (v) ....

doorway (n) ....

expression (n) ....

fight (fought – fought) (v) ....

fight (n) ....

footsteps (n, pl) ....

fresh air (phr) ....

go on (went – gone) (phr v) ....

honest (adj) ....

in private (phr) ....

keep in the shadows (phr) ....

manage (v) ....

mark (n) ....

nail (n) ....

pool (n) ....

roll down (v) ....

scream (v) ....

share (v) ....

solve (v) ....

strike (struke – struck) (v) ....

swear (swore – sworn) (v) ....

Take no notice of her. (exp) ....

Chapter 10

abroad (adv) ....

adopt (v) ....

angrily (adv) ....

arrest (v) ....

be after sb (phr) ....

belong to (v) ....

break sth down (broke – broken) (phr v) ....

chest (n) ....

chimney (n) ....

crime (n) ....

curse (n) ....

eventually (adv) ....

fair (adj) ....

free (adj) ....

friendship (n) ....

fur (n) ....

guilty (adj) ....

happiness (n) ....

howl (n) ....

hunt down (phr v) ....

in fact (phr) ....

justice is served (exp) ....

member (n) ....

monster (n) ....

murder (n) ....

papers (n, pl) ....

prison (n) ....

roof (n) ....

rope (n) ....

sign (v) ....

thanks to sb (phr) ....

tighten (v) ....

trial (n) ....

wicked (adj) ....

You have my word as a gentleman. (exp) ....